SMOKER COOKBOOK

COMPLETE SMOKER COOKBOOK FOR REAL BARBECUE,
THE ART OF SMOKING MEAT FOR REAL PITMASTERS,
THE ULTIMATE HOW-TO GUIDE FOR SMOKING MEAT

BY GARY MERCER

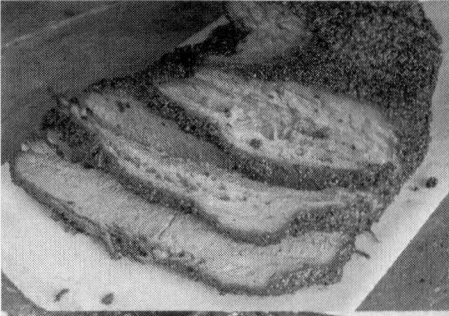

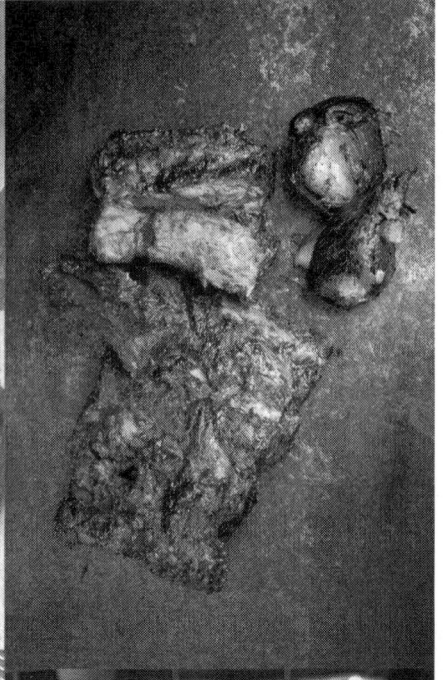

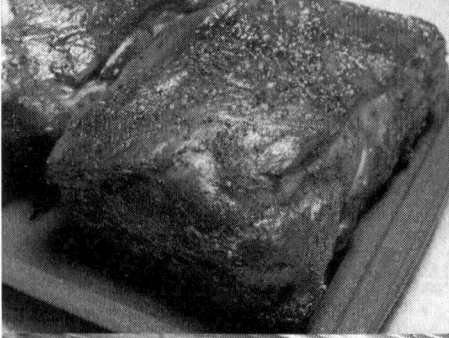

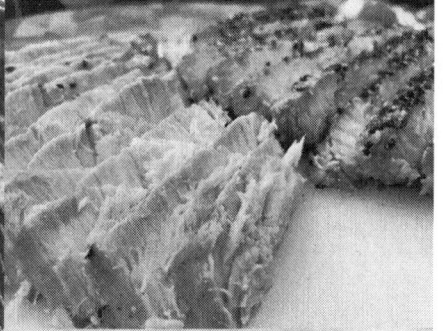

2

Table of Contents

Why Smoking **6**

Chapter-1 Smoking Tips and Tricks **8**

Selecting a Smoker **8**

Choose your wood..........................**9**

Select the right meat **11**

Find the right temperature **11**

Chapter-2 BEEF **12**

Chipotle Brisket **12**

Oregano Tri-Tip............................**15**

Smoked Burgers............................**17**

Beef Loaf **19**

Sweet Ribs.................................**22**

Chapter-3 FISH AND SEAFOOD **25**

Salmon Nuggets..........................**25**

Tuna Steak...28

Shrimps 32

Crab Legs 34

Oyster Tender...36

Trout in Orange Aroma 39

Sweet Squids 42

Snapper 44

Chapter-4 Pork............................47

Pork Ribs with Black Pepper 47

Pork Tenderloin 50

Brown Smoked Pork 53

Pulled Pork 56

Pork Shoulder 59

Chapter-5 Poultry 62

Whole Turkey 62

Chicken Breast with Wine 65

Goose Breast 68

Honey Duck with Black Tea 71

Chicken with Coffee and Berries 74

Chapter-6 GAME 77

Pheasant with Maple Syrup 77

Moist Elk Loin 80

Venison in Mushroom Sauce..................83

Spiced Grouse...86

Chapter-7 VEGETABLES 89

Carrots..89

Cauliflower 92

Mixed Vegetables 95

Conclusion 98

Other books by Gary Mercer 99

WHY SMOKING

The ultimate how-to guide for smoking all types of meat, poultry, fish, and game. This book on smoking meats for beginners is the guide to mastering the low and slow art of smoking beef, fish, seafood, poultry, pork, vegetables, and game at your home. This guide is an essential book for beginners who want to smoke meat without needing expert help from others. This book offers detailed guidance obtained by years of smoking meat, includes clear instructions and step-by-step directions for every recipe. This is the only guide you will ever need to professionally smoke a variety of meat. From well-known beef brisket, the book includes delicate elk, turkey, venison, and pheasant smoked meat recipes.

The book includes photographs of every finished meal to make your job easier. Whether you are a beginner meat smoker or looking to go beyond the basics, the book gives you the tools and tips you need to start that perfectly smoked meat. Smoking is generally used as one of the cooking methods now days. The food enrich in protein such as meat would spoil quickly, if cooked for a longer period of time with modern cooking techniques. Whereas, Smoking is a low & slow process of cooking the meat. Where there is a smoke, there is a flavor. With white smoke, you can boost the flavor of your food. In addition to this statement, you can preserve the nutrition present inside the food as well. This is flexible & one of the oldest techniques of making food. It's essential for you to brush the marinade over your food while you cook and let the miracle happen. The only thing you need to do is to add a handful of fresh coals or wood chips as and when required. Just taste your regular grilled meat and a smoked meat, you yourself would find the difference. Remember one thing i.e. "Smoking is an art". With a little time & practice even you can become an expert. Once you become an expert with smoking technique, believe me you would never look for other cooking techniques. To find one which smoking technique works for you, you must experiment with different woods & cooking methods. Just cook the meat over indirect heat source & cook it for hours. When smoking your meats, it's very important that you let the smoke to escape & move around.

CHAPTER-1 SMOKING TIPS AND TRICKS

Before starting the recipes, let's discuss a few tips and tricks about smoking meats.

SELECTING A SMOKER

You need to invest in a good smoker if you are going to smoke meat on a regular basis. Consider these options when buying a smoker. Here are two natural fire option for you:

- Charcoal smokers are fueled with a combination of charcoal and wood. Charcoal burns easily and the temperature remains steady, so you won't have any problem with a charcoal smoker. The wood gives a great flavor to the meat and you will enjoy smoking meats.

- Wood smoker: The wood smoker will give your brisket and ribs the best smoky flavor and taste, but it is a bit harder to cook with wood. Both hardwood blocks and chips are used as fuel.

CHOOSE YOUR WOOD

You need to choose your wood carefully because the type of wood you will use affect greatly to the flavor and taste of the meat. Here are a few options for you:

- Maple: Maple has a smoky and sweet taste and goes well with pork or poultry

- Alder: Alder is sweet and light. Perfect for poultry and fish.

- Apple: Apple has a mild and sweet flavor. Goes well with pork, fish, and poultry.

- Oak: Oak is great for slow cooking. Ideal for game, pork, beef, and lamb.

- Mesquite: Mesquite has a smoky flavor and extremely strong. Goes well with pork or beef.

- Hickory: Has a smoky and strong flavor. Goes well with beef and lamb.

- Cherry Has a mild and sweet flavor. Great for pork, beef, and turkey

To cook the meat, you may refer the below mentioned chart that can help you with selecting the best wood chips/chunks

Remember, black smoke is bad and white smoke is good. Ensue proper ventilation for great tasting smoked meat.

Wood Type	Lamb	Chicken	Beef	Pork
Apple	Yes	Yes	No	No
Alder	Yes	Yes	No	Yes
Cherry	Yes	Yes	Yes	Yes
Hickory	No	No	Yes	Yes
Maple	No	Yes	No	No
Mulberry	Yes	Yes	No	Yes
Mesquite	No	No	Yes	Yes
Oak	Yes	Yes	Yes	Yes
Pecan	No	Yes	Yes	Yes
Pear	No	Yes	No	Yes
Peach	No	Yes	No	Yes
Walnut	No	No	Yes	Yes

SELECT THE RIGHT MEAT

Some meats are just ideal for the smoking process, including:

- Chicken

- Turkey

- Pork roast

- Ham

- Brisket

- Pork and beef ribs

- Corned beef

FIND THE RIGHT TEMPERATURE

- Start at 250F (120C): Start your smoker a bit hot. This extra heat gets the smoking process going.

- Temperature drop: Once you add the meat to the smoker, the temperature will drop, which is fine.

- Maintain the temperature. Monitor and maintain the temperature. Keep the temperature steady during the smoking process.

Avoid peeking every now and then. Smoke and heat two most important element makes your meat taste great. If you open the cover every now and then you lose both of them and your meat lose flavor. Only the lid only when you truly need it.

CHAPTER-2 BEEF

CHIPOTLE BRISKET

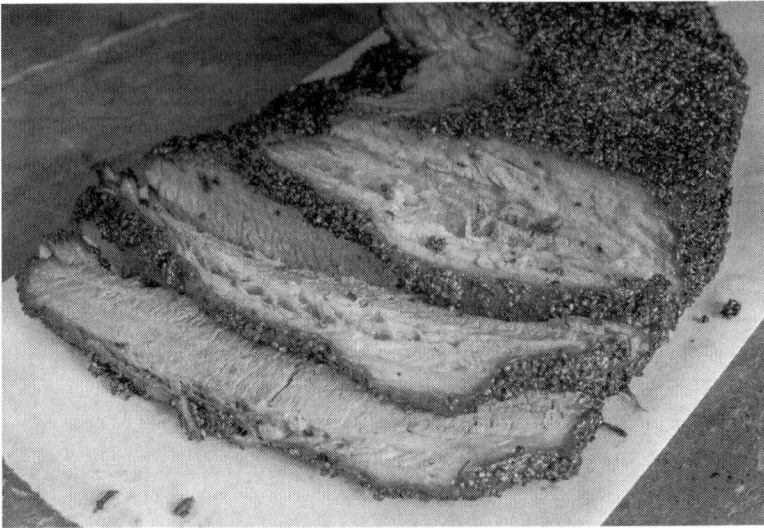

(TOTAL COOK TIME 29 HOURS 10 MINUTES)

INGREDIENTS FOR 10 SERVINGS

- Beef Brisket (6-lbs., 2.7-kgs)

THE RUB

- Chipotle powder – 2 teaspoons
- Olive oil – 3 teaspoons

- Black pepper – 1 ½ tablespoons

- Salt – 1 ½ tablespoons

- Brown sugar – 1 ½ teaspoons

- Onion powder – 1 ½ teaspoons

- Garlic powder – 1 teaspoon

- Dry mustard – 1 teaspoon

- Chili powder – 1 teaspoon

THE GLAZE

- Low sodium beef broth – 2 tablespoons

- Unsweetened apple juice – 3 tablespoons

- BBQ sauce – 3 tablespoons

THE FIRE

- Preheat the smoker an hour prior to smoking.

- Add charcoal and hickory chips during the smoking time.

THE METHOD

1. Combine chipotle powder with black pepper, salt, brown sugar, onion powder, garlic powder, dry mustard, and chili powder in a bowl.

2. Add olive oil to the bowl then stir until mixed.

3. Rub the beef brisket with the spice mixture then marinated for 24 hours. Chill in refrigerator to keep it fresh.

4. After 24 hours, take the marinated beef brisket out from the refrigerator then thaw   until it reaches the room temperature.

5. Place charcoal and hickory wood chips in the smoker then preheat the smoker to 225 °F (107°C)—using indirect heat.

6. When the smoker has reached the desired temperature, place the beef brisket in the smoker.

7. Smoke the beef brisket until the internal temperature is 150°F (66°C).

8. Take the beef brisket out from the smoker then transfer the half-smoked beef brisket to a pan.

9. Combine low sodium beef broth with unsweetened apple juice then pour the mixture over the beef brisket.

10. Wrap the pan with aluminum foil then return to the smoker.

11. Smoke the beef brisket for 3 hours then check the internal temperature. It should have reached 190°F (88°C).

12. Remove the pan from the smoker then transfer the smoked beef brisket to a serving dish.

13. Drizzle BBQ sauce on top then serve.

OREGANO TRI-TIP

(TOTAL COOK TIME 2 HOURS 10 MINUTES)

INGREDIENTS FOR 10 SERVINGS

- Beef tri-tip (6-lbs., 2.7-kgs)

THE RUB

- Olive oil - 1 tablespoon
- Salt – 3 tablespoons
- Chipotle – 1 ½ tablespoons
- Oregano – 1 ½ tablespoons

15

- Garlic powder – 1 tablespoon

- Cumin 1 ½ tablespoons

- Black pepper – 1 tablespoon

THE FIRE

- Preheat the smoker an hour prior to smoking.

- Add charcoal and use mesquite chips during the smoking time.

THE METHOD

1. Preheat a smoker to 225°F (107°C). Don't forget to soak the mesquite wood chips before using.

2. Place chipotle in a bowl then add salt, oregano, garlic powder, cumin, and black pepper. Mix well.

3. Coat the beef tri-tip with olive oil then rub with the spice mixture.

4. Place the tri-tip in a smoker then smoke for an hour and 45 minutes.

5. Check if the internal temperature has reached 130°F (54°C) then remove from the smoker.

6. Place the smoked beef tri-tip on a flat surface then cut into slices.

7. Arrange the sliced smoked beef on a serving dish then enjoy.

8. Sprinkle salsa over the smoked beef if you like.

SMOKED BURGERS

(TOTAL COOK TIME 2 HOURS 10 MINUTES)

INGREDIENTS FOR 10 SERVINGS

- Ground beef (2.5-lbs., 1.1-kgs)

THE RUB

- Salt – 1 teaspoon

- Pepper – 1 teaspoon

THE FIRE

- Preheat the smoker an hour prior to smoking.

- Add charcoal and use hickory wood chips during the smoking time.

THE METHOD

1. Preheat a smoker to 225°F (107°C) and coat a disposable aluminum pan with cooking spray.

2. Season the ground beef with salt and pepper then mix until combined.

3. Shape the seasoned ground beef into 8 patties then arrange the patties in the aluminum pan.

4. Place the pan in the smoker then smoke the beef patties for approximately 2 hours. The internal temperature should have reached 130°F (54°C).

5. Remove the pan from the smoker then transfer the patties to a serving dish.

6. Serve and enjoy with burger buns and your desired topping.

BEEF LOAF

(TOTAL COOK TIME 4 HOURS 30 MINUTES)

INGREDIENTS FOR 10 SERVINGS

- Ground beef (5-lbs., 2.3-kgs)

THE SPICES

- Olive oil – ¼ cup

- Chopped onion – 2 cups

- Chopped celeries – 1 cup

- Diced bell pepper – 1 cup

- Minced jalapeno – 3 tablespoons

- Breadcrumbs – ½ cup

- Buttermilk – 1 ½ cups

- Worcestershire sauce – ¼ cup

- Organic eggs – 4

THE GLAZE

- BBQ Sauce – 3 cups

THE FIRE

- Preheat the smoker an hour prior to smoking.

- Add charcoal and use cherry wood chips during the smoking time.

- Soak the wood chips before using.

THE METHOD

1. Preheat a smoker to 225°F (107°C) and coat a disposable aluminum pan with cooking spray.

2. Preheat a skillet over medium heat pour olive oil into the skillet.

3. Stir in chopped onion then sauté until aromatic and translucent. Remove from heat then set aside.

4. Place ground beef in a bowl then add chopped celeries, diced bell peppers, minced jalapeno,

breadcrumbs, buttermilk, Worcestershire sauce, and then sauté onion. Mix well.

5. Crack the eggs then place in another bowl. Stir until incorporated.

6. Pour the beaten eggs into the ground beef mixture then mix until combined.

7. Transfer the ground beef mixture to the prepared disposable aluminum pan then spread evenly.

8. Once the smoker has reached the desired temperature, place the disposable aluminum pan in the smoker.

9. Smoke the loaf for approximately 3 hours or until the internal temperature has reached 150°F (66°C).

10. Remove the smoked loaf from the smoker then increase the temperature of the smoker to 350°F (177°C).

11. Glaze the smoked loaf with BBQ sauce then return it back to the smoker.

12. Smoke the glazed loaf for approximately an hour or until the internal temperature has reached 160°F (71°C).

13. Take the smoked loaf out of the smoker then let it sit for about 10 minutes.

14. Cut the smoked loaf into slices then serve.

Sweet Ribs

(TOTAL COOK TIME **3** HOURS **20** MINUTES)

INGREDIENTS FOR **10** SERVINGS

- Beef ribs (5-lbs., 2.3-kgs)

THE RUBS

- Salt – 1 tablespoon

- Black pepper – ¾ tablespoon

- Onion powder – 1 teaspoon

- Garlic powder – 1 teaspoon

THE GLAZE

- Ketchup – 1 ¼ cups

- Applesauce – 1 cup

- Steak sauce – ¾ cup

- Brown sugar – 5 tablespoons

THE FIRE

- Preheat the smoker an hour prior to smoking.

- Add charcoal and use hickory wood chips during the smoking time.

- Soak the wood chips before using.

THE METHOD

1. Preheat a smoker to 225°F (107°C)—use indirect heat and don't forget to soak the hickory wood chips before using.

2. Place salt, black pepper, onion powder, and garlic powder in a bowl then mix well.

3. Rub the beef ribs with the spice mixture then let it sit while waiting for the smoker.

4. Once the smoker is ready, place the beef ribs in the smoker and smoke for approximately an hour.

5. Meanwhile, pour ketchup, applesauce, and steak sauce into a saucepan then add the brown sugar. Stir well and bring to a simmer.

6. Remove the half-smoked beef ribs from the smoker then glaze with the applesauce mixture.

7. Wrap the glazed beef ribs with aluminum foil then return it back to the smoker.

8. Smoke the wrapped beef ribs for 3 hours or until the internal temperature has reached 165°F (174°C).

9. Once it is done, remove from the smoker then serve.

CHAPTER-3 FISH AND SEAFOOD

SALMON NUGGETS

(TOTAL COOK TIME 26 HOURS 10 MINUTES)

INGREDIENTS FOR 10 SERVINGS

- Salmon fillets (2-lbs., 0.9-kgs)

THE SPICE

- Maple syrup – 1 ½ cups

- Salt – ¼ cup

- Fish sauce – 3 tablespoons

- Black pepper – 2 teaspoons

- Chipotle – 1 teaspoon

- Minced garlic – 3 teaspoons

THE GLAZE

- Maple syrup – ½ cup

THE FIRE

- Preheat the smoker an hour prior to smoking.

- Add charcoal and maple wood chips during the smoking time.

THE METHOD

1. Cut the salmon fillets into cubes then place in a zipper-lock plastic bag.

2. Combine maple syrup with salt, fish sauce, chipotle, minced garlic, and black pepper then mix well.

3. Pour the spice mixture over the salmon cubes then seal the plastic bag properly.

4. Shake the plastic bag until all the salmon cubes are completely coated with the spices.

5. Marinate the salmon cubes for 24 hours and place in the fridge to keep them fresh.

6. After 24 hours, prepare a smoker and preheat to 225°F (107°C).

7. Remove the marinated salmon cubes out of the fridge then thaw to room temperature.

8. Wash and rinse the marinated salmon cubes then arrange on the smoker's grill.

9. Smoke the salmon cubes for 2 hours. Baste the salmon with maple syrup once every 20 minutes.

10. Once it is done, remove the smoked salmon from the smoker then transfer to a serving dish.

11. Serve and enjoy warm.

TUNA STEAK

(TOTAL COOK TIME 6 HOURS 10 MINUTES)

INGREDIENTS FOR 10 SERVINGS

- Tuna steak (5-lbs., 2.3-kgs)

THE MARINATE

- Salt – ½ cup
- Brown sugar – 2 cups
- Bay leaves – 2 teaspoons

- Lemon juice – ½ cup

- White wine – 3 cups

THE GLAZE

- Olive oil – ¼ cup

THE TOPPING

- Sesame seeds – 3 tablespoons

THE FIRE

- Preheat the smoker an hour prior to smoking.

- Add charcoal and apple wood chips during the smoking time.

- Soak the wood chips before using.

THE METHOD

1. Place salt, brown sugar, and bay leaves in a zipper-lock plastic bag then stir well.

2. Pour lemon juice and white wine into the mixture then mix well.

3. Add the tuna steaks to the plastic bag then seal it properly.

4. Shake the plastic bag to ensure that all parts of the tuna are completely seasoned.

5. Marinate the tuna for 3 hours and chill in the fridge to keep it fresh.

6. After 3 hours, remove the marinated tuna from the fridge then transfer to a disposable aluminum pan.

7. Glaze the tuna with olive oil then set aside.

8. Preheat a smoker to 225°F (107°C)—using indirect heat with charcoal and soaked apple wood chips.

9. When the smoker is ready, place the disposable aluminum pan on the smoker's rack.

10. Smoke the tuna steak for 3 hours or until the tuna easily flakes.

11. Remove from the smoker then transfer to a serving dish together with the liquid.

12. Sprinkle sesame seeds on top then serve.

13. Combine maple syrup with salt, fish sauce, chipotle, minced garlic, and black pepper then mix well.

14. Pour the spice mixture over the salmon cubes then seal the plastic bag properly.

15. Shake the plastic bag until all the salmon cubes are completely coated with the spices.

16. Marinate the salmon cubes for 24 hours and place in the fridge to keep them fresh.

17. After 24 hours, prepare a smoker and preheat to 225°F (107°C).

18. Remove the marinated salmon cubes out of the fridge then thaw to room temperature.

19. Wash and rinse the marinated salmon cubes then arrange on the smoker's grill.

20. Smoke the salmon cubes for 2 hours. Baste the salmon with maple syrup once every 20 minutes.

21. Once it is done, remove the smoked salmon from the smoker then transfer to a serving dish.

22. Serve and enjoy warm.

SHRIMPS

(TOTAL COOK TIME 30 MINUTES)

INGREDIENTS FOR 10 SERVINGS

- Fresh shrimps (5-lbs., 2.3-kgs)

THE RUB

- Garlic powder – 2 tablespoons
- Salt – 1 tablespoon
- Black pepper – 1 teaspoon

THE GLAZE

- Butter – 1 cup
- Minced garlic – 2 tablespoons

The Fire

- Preheat the smoker an hour prior to smoking.

- Add charcoal and cherry wood chips during the smoking time.

- Soak the wood chips before using.

The Method

1. Preheat a smoker to 225°F (107°C)—using indirect heat with charcoal and soaked cherry wood chips.

2. Peel the fresh shrimps and discard the head.

3. Place the peeled fresh shrimps in a disposable aluminum pan then sprinkle salt, garlic powder, and black pepper over the shrimps. Toss to combine.

4. Once the smoker has reached the desired temperature, place the disposable aluminum pan in the smoker.

5. Smoke the shrimps for 20-25 minutes until the shrimps are cooked through.

6. Meanwhile, melt butter over low heat then stir in minced garlic. Mix well.

7. After 10 minutes, drizzle the melted butter over shrimps then continue smoking according to the suggested time.

8. Once it is done, remove the smoked shrimps from the smoker then transfer to a serving dish.

9. Serve and enjoy.

CRAB LEGS

(TOTAL COOK TIME 30 MINUTES)

INGREDIENTS FOR 10 SERVINGS

- Frozen Crab Legs (6-lbs., 2.7-kgs)

THE GLAZE

- Minced garlic – ½ cup
- Italian parsley – ¼ cup
- Lemon juice – ¼ cup
- Olive oil – ½ cup
- Cayenne pepper – 3 tablespoons

THE FIRE

- Preheat the smoker an hour prior to smoking.

- Add charcoal and cherry wood chips during the smoking time.

- Soak the wood chips before using.

THE METHOD

1. Preheat a smoker to 225°F (107°C)—using indirect heat with charcoal and soaked cherry wood chips.

2. Preheat a skillet over medium heat then pour olive oil into the skillet.

3. Stir in minced garlic then sauté until wilted and aromatic. Remove from heat.

4. Add Italian parsley, lemon juice, and cayenne pepper then stir well.

5. Place the crab legs in a disposable aluminum pan then drizzle the garlic mixture over the crab legs.

6. Smoke the crab legs for 25 minutes then remove from the smoker.

7. Arrange the crab legs on a serving dish then serve.

8. Enjoy warm.

OYSTER TENDER

(TOTAL COOK TIME 25 HOURS 40 MINUTES)

INGREDIENTS FOR 10 SERVINGS

- Fresh Oyster (3-lbs., 1.4-kgs)

THE BRINE

- Salt – ½ cup

- Brown sugar – 1 ¼ cups

- Soy sauce – ½ cup

- Bay leaves – 2

- Garlic powder – 1 ½ tablespoons

- Brandy – ¾ cup

- Pepper – ½ teaspoon

- Onion powder – 1 teaspoon

- Water

THE FIRE

- Preheat the smoker an hour prior to smoking.

- Add charcoal and hickory wood chips during the smoking time.

- Soak the wood chips before using.

THE METHOD

1. Place salt, brown sugar, soy sauce, bay leaves, pepper, garlic powder, and onion powder in a pot.

2. Pour soy sauce, brandy, and water then stir until the dry ingredients are completely dissolved.

3. Add the oysters to the brine and soak for 24 hours. Chill in the fridge to keep them fresh.

4. After 24 hours, remove the oysters from the refrigerator then wash and rinse them completely. Place on a grill rack.

5. Preheat a smoker to 225°F (107°C).

6. When the smoker is ready, smoke the oysters for an hour and a half.

7. Once it is done, remove from the smoked oysters from the smoker and transfer to a serving dish.

8. Enjoy right away.

Trout in Orange Aroma

(TOTAL COOK TIME 24 HOURS 40 MINUTES)

INGREDIENTS FOR 10 SERVINGS

- Trout (5-lbs., 2.3-kgs)

THE RUB

- Brown sugar – 2 cups
- Salt – ¾ cup
- Pepper – 2 ½ teaspoons

- Thyme – 1 teaspoon

- Bay leaves – 2

- Grated orange zest – 3 teaspoons

- Unsweetened orange juice – 2 cups

THE FIRE

- Preheat the smoker an hour prior to smoking.

- Add charcoal and hickory wood chips during the smoking time.

- Soak the wood chips before using.

THE METHOD

1. Combine brown sugar, salt, pepper, thyme, and grated orange zest in a bowl.

2. Pour orange juice over the dry mixture then stir until incorporated.

3. Add bay leaves to the mixture then mix well.

4. Rub the trout with the spice mixture then marinate overnight. Store in the refrigerator to keep the trout fresh.

5. After 24 hours, prepare a smoker and preheat it to 22s°F (107°C)—use soaked hickory wood chips.

6. Take the trout out from the refrigerator then rinse it completely. Arrange in a disposable aluminum pan.

7. When the smoker has reached the desired temperature, place the disposable aluminum pan in the smoker.

8. Smoke the trout for approximately 30 minutes or until the trout is easy to flake.

9. Once it is done, remove from the smoker and transfer to a serving dish.

10. Serve and enjoy.

Sweet Squids

(TOTAL COOK TIME 40 MINUTES)

INGREDIENTS FOR 10 SERVINGS

- Squids (5-lbs., 2.3-kgs)

THE BRINE

- Brown sugar – 3 cups
- Water – 1 ½ cups

THE FIRE

- Preheat the smoker an hour prior to smoking.

- Add charcoal and apple wood chips during the smoking time.

- Soak the wood chips before using.

THE METHOD

1. Preheat a smoker to 225°F (107°C).

2. Place brown sugar and water in a container then stir until the sugar is completely dissolved.

3. Add squids to the brown sugar mixture then soak for about 20 minutes.

4. After 20 minutes, take the squids out of the brine then drain them completely.

5. Arrange the squids on the smoker's rack and smoke for 10-15 minutes.

6. Once it is done, remove from the smoker and arrange the smoked squids on a serving dish.

7. Serve and enjoy!

SNAPPER

(TOTAL COOK TIME 40 MINUTES)

INGREDIENTS FOR 10 SERVINGS

- Red snappers (5-lbs., 2.3-kgs)

THE RUB

- Salt – ½ cup
- Black pepper – 2 tablespoons
- Cilantro – ½ cup
- Grated ginger – ½ cup
- Garlic powder – 3 tablespoons

- Coconut milk – 2 cups

- Rum – ¾ cup

- Lemon juice – ¼ cup

- Brown sugar – ¼ cup

THE FIRE

- Olive oil – ½ cup

THE FIRE

- Preheat the smoker an hour prior to smoking.

- Add charcoal and Mesquite wood chips during the smoking time.

- Soak the wood chips before using.

THE METHOD

1. Diagonally cut the red snappers in several places.

2. Place salt, black pepper, cilantro, ginger, garlic powder, and brown sugar in a zipper-lock plastic bag.

3. Pour coconut milk, rum, and lemon juice into the plastic bag then mix well.

4. Add the red snappers to the zipper-lock plastic bag then seal it properly. Shake to ensure that the red snappers are completely coated with spice mixture.

5. Marinate the red snappers for 2 hours and it is better to chill them in the fridge. This will help to keep the fish fresh.

6. Preheat a smoker to 225°F (107°C).

7. After 2 hours, take the red snappers out of the fridge then arrange in a disposable aluminum pan.

8. Once the smoker is ready, place the pan in the smoker and smoke the red snappers for an hour or until the fish flakes easily. Baste with olive oil once every 10 minutes.

9. Remove the smoked red snappers from the smoker then quickly wrap with aluminum foil. Let it sit for 15 minutes.

10. After 15 minutes, unwrap the smoked red snappers then arrange on a serving dish.

11. Garnish with sliced lemon then serve.

12. Enjoy!

CHAPTER-4 PORK

PORK RIBS WITH BLACK PEPPER

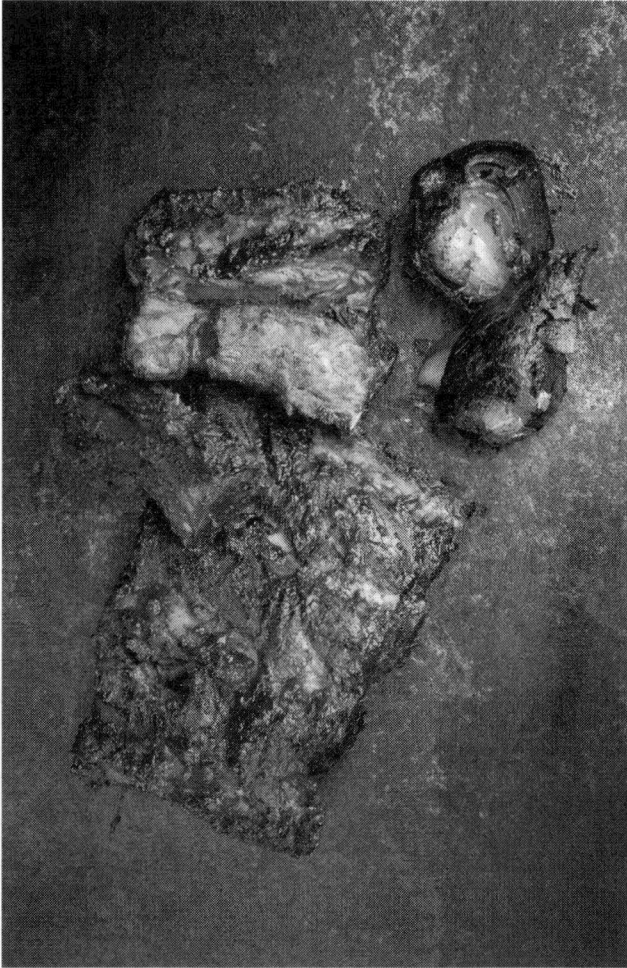

(TOTAL COOK TIME 30 HOURS 10 MINUTES)

INGREDIENTS FOR 10 SERVINGS

- Baby Pork Ribs (10-lbs., 4.5-kgs)

THE RUB

- Salt – ¼ cup

- Brown sugar – ¼ cup

- Chili powder – 2 tablespoons

- Onion powder – ¾ tablespoon

- Garlic powder – ¾ tablespoon

- Black pepper – 1 ¼ teaspoons

- Cumin – 1 teaspoon

- Coriander – ½ teaspoon

THE FIRE

- Preheat the smoker an hour prior to smoking.

- Add charcoal and peach wood chips during the smoking time.

- Soak the wood chips before using.

THE METHOD

1. Place salt, brown sugar, chili powder, onion powder, garlic powder, black pepper, cumin, and coriander then stir well.

2. Rub the pork ribs with the spice mixture then marinate for 24 hours. Chill in the refrigerator to keep it fresh.

3. After 24 hours, take the pork ribs out of the refrigerator then thaw to room temperature. Place in a disposable aluminum pan.

4. Place charcoal and peach wood chips in the smoker then preheat the smoker to 225 °F (107°C)—using indirect heat.

5. Place the disposable aluminum pan in the smoker then smoke for 5 hours.

6. Once the internal temperature has reached 165°F (174°C), remove the aluminum pan from the smoker.

7. Transfer the smoked pork ribs to a serving dish then enjoy.

PORK TENDERLOIN

(TOTAL COOK TIME 3 HOURS 10 MINUTES)

INGREDIENTS FOR 10 SERVINGS

- Pork Tenderloin (5-lbs., 2.3-kgs)

THE RUB

- Olive oil – ¼ cup

- Dijon mustard – 3 tablespoons

- Minced garlic – 3 tablespoons

- Black pepper – 1 teaspoon

- Fresh rosemary – 20 sprigs

THE FIRE

- Preheat the smoker an hour prior to smoking.

- Add charcoal and nectarine wood chips during the smoking time.

- Soak the wood chips before using.

THE METHOD

1. Place charcoal and nectarine wood chips in the smoker then preheat the smoker to 225 °F (107°C)—using indirect heat.

2. Combine Dijon mustard, minced garlic, and black pepper in a bowl.

3. Pour olive oil over the spice mixture then mix well.

4. Rub the pork tenderloin with the spice mixture then arrange fresh rosemary over the pork tenderloin. Using a kitchen string tie the rosemary with the tenderloin.

5. When the smoker has reached the desired temperature, place the pork tenderloin in the smoker.

6. Smoke the pork tenderloin for approximately 3 hours. Flip the pork tenderloin once every hour.

7. When the internal temperature reaches 145•F (63°C), remove the smoked pork tenderloin from the smoker.

8. Let it sit for about 5 minutes then remove the string from the smoked pork tenderloin.

9. Cut the smoked pork tenderloin into slices then serve.

Brown Smoked Pork

(total cook time 9 hours 20 minutes)

Ingredients for 10 servings

- Pork butt (5-lbs., 2.3-kgs)

The Injection

- Unsweetened apple juice – 1 ¼ cups

- Water – 1 ¼ cups

- Brown sugar – ¾ cup

- Salt – ½ cup

- Low sodium soy sauce – 1 ½ tablespoons

- Worcestershire sauce – 1 ½ tablespoons

THE RUB

- Olive oil – 1 cup

- Apple cider vinegar – 1 cup

- Water – 1 cup

- BBQ rub – 1 cup

- Worcestershire sauce – 2 ½ tablespoons

- Low sodium soy sauce – 2 ½ tablespoons

THE GLAZE

- BBQ Sauce – 1 ½ cups

THE FIRE

- Preheat the smoker an hour prior to smoking.

- Add charcoal and use plum wood chips during the smoking time.

- Soak the wood chips before using.

THE METHOD

1. Combine unsweetened apple juice with water then add brown sugar, salt, soy sauce, and

Worcestershire sauce in a bowl. Stir until incorporated.

2. Place the pork butt in a disposable aluminum pan then inject the mixture into the pork butt. Inject the pork butt on all sides.

3. Place the injected pork butt in a zipper-lock plastic bag then marinate for 4 hours. Store in the refrigerator for at least 4 hours.

4. After 4 hours, preheat a smoker to 225°F (107°C)—use indirect heat and don't forget to soak the plum wood chips before using.

5. While waiting for the smoker, combine the rub ingredients in a bowl then mix well.

6. Rub the pork butt with the spice mixture then smoke for 4 hours or until the internal temperature reaches 195°F (90°C).

7. Take the smoked pork butt out from the smoker then carefully unwrap it.

8. Discard the liquid from the smoked pork butt then re-wrap with a new aluminum foil.

9. Let the wrapped smoked beef sit for at least 4 hours then unwrap it.

10. Preheat the smoker again to 245°F (118°C).

11. Glaze the smoked pork butt with BBQ sauce then smoke for an hour.

12. Once it is done, remove from the smoker then let it sit for a few minutes.

13. Cut the smoked pork butt into slices then serve.

PULLED PORK

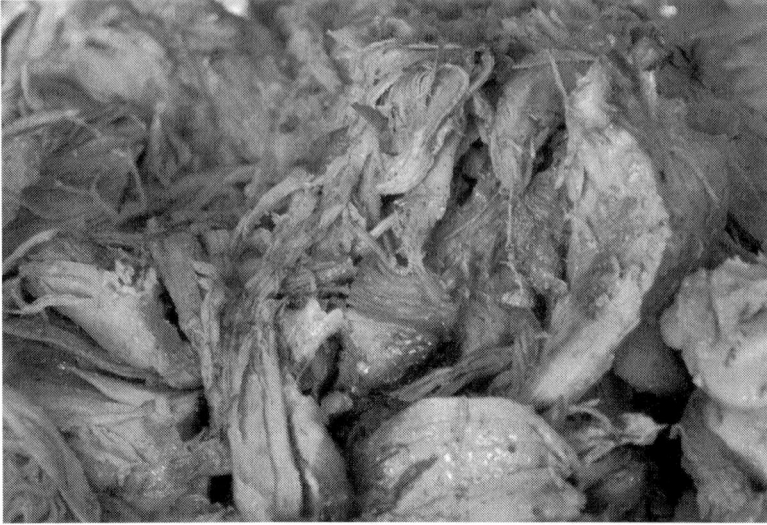

(TOTAL COOK TIME 10 HOURS 20 MINUTES)

INGREDIENTS FOR 10 SERVINGS

- Pork shoulder (5-lbs., 2.3-kgs)

THE RUB

- Chopped onion – ½ cup

- Ketchup – ¾ ketchup

- Barbecue seasoning – 3 tablespoons

- Cider vinegar – ¼ cup

- Brown sugar – ½ cup

- Tomato puree – ½ cup

- Sweet paprika – 2 ½ tablespoons

- Worcestershire sauce – 3 tablespoons

- Salt – ½ tablespoon

- Black pepper – 1 ½ teaspoons

THE FIRE

- Preheat the smoker an hour prior to smoking.

- Add charcoal and use hickory wood chips during the smoking time.

- Soak the wood chips before using.

THE METHOD

1. Preheat a smoker to 225°F (107°C)—use indirect heat and don't forget to soak the hickory wood chips before using.

2. Combine ketchup with barbecue seasoning, cider vinegar, tomato puree, and Worcestershire sauce. Stir until incorporated.

3. Add chopped onion, brown sugar, sweet paprika, salt, and black pepper then mix well.

4. Rub the pork shoulder with the spice mixture then wrap with aluminum foil. Prick the aluminum foil in several places to help the smoke get into the pork shoulder.

5. Once the smoker is ready, place the wrapped pork shoulder in the smoker.

6. Smoke the pork shoulder for 10 hours and check the smoke and the wood chips once every 2 hours. Add more soaked wood chips if it is necessary.

7. When the internal temperature has reached 195°F (90°C), remove the smoked pork shoulder from the smoker.

8. Let the smoked pork shoulder sit for a few minutes then unwrap it.

9. Shred the smoked pork shoulder then place on a serving dish.

10. Serve and enjoy.

Pork Shoulder

(TOTAL COOK TIME 14 HOURS 10 MINUTES)

INGREDIENTS FOR 10 SERVINGS

- Pork shoulder (5-lbs., 2.3-kgs)

THE RUB

- Chinese five-spice – 3 tablespoons

THE MARINATE

- Hoisin sauce – ¾ cup
- Raw honey – ¾ cup

- Soy sauce -1/2 cup

- Dry Sherry – ¼ cup

- Chinese five-spice – ¾ tablespoon

THE FIRE

- Preheat the smoker an hour prior to smoking.

- Add charcoal and use hickory wood chips during the smoking time.

- Soak the wood chips before using.

THE METHOD

1. Rub the pork shoulder with the Chinese five-spice then place in a zipper-lock plastic bag.

2. Place Hoisin sauce, raw honey, soy sauce, dry sherry, and Chinese five-spice in a bowl then mix well.

3. Pour the Hoisin mixture into the zipper-lock plastic bag with pork shoulder then shake until the pork is completely coated with the Hoisin sauce mixture.

4. Marinate the pork shoulder for overnight. Store in the fridge to keep it fresh.

5. In the morning, remove the pork from the fridge then thaw to room temperature.

6. Preheat a smoker to 225°F (107°C)—use indirect heat and don't forget to soak the hickory wood chips before using.

7. Once the smoker has reached the desired temperature, place the marinated pork shoulder in the smoker. Reserve the liquid.

8. Smoke the pork shoulder for 5 hours and check the wood chips if it is necessary.

9. Meanwhile, pour the hoisin sauce mixture into a saucepan then bring to a simmer. Remove from heat.

10. After 5 hours, take the smoked pork out of the smoker then brush with the liquid.

11. Place the glazed smoked pork in a disposable aluminum pan then return it back to the smoker.

12. Smoke for an hour then remove from the smoker. The internal temperature should be 195°F (90°C).

13. Cut the smoked pork into thick slices then serve.

CHAPTER-5 POULTRY

WHOLE TURKEY

(TOTAL COOK TIME 29 HOURS 30 MINUTES)

INGREDIENTS FOR 10 SERVINGS

- Whole turkey (6-lbs., 2.7-kgs)

THE BRINE

- Water – 2 ½ quarts
- Salt – 1 ½ cups

- Maple syrup – 1 cup

- Chopped thyme – 1 ½ teaspoons

- Bay leaves – 4 sprigs

- Minced garlic – 3 teaspoons

THE FIRE

- Preheat the smoker an hour prior to smoking.

- Add charcoal and maple wood chips during the smoking time.

- Soak the wood chips before using.

THE METHOD

1. Pour water into a large container then stir in salt, maple syrup, thyme, bay leaves, and minced garlic. Mix until the salt is completely dissolved.

2. Add the turkey into the container then soak for 24 hours. Chill in the refrigerator to keep it fresh.

3. After 24 hours, take the turkey out of the refrigerator then discard the brine.

4. Place charcoal and maple wood chips in the smoker then preheat the smoker to 225 °F (107°C)—using indirect heat.

5. Place the turkey in a pan then smoke for 5 hours. Check the smoke and the wood chip regularly.

6. Once the internal temperature has reached 165°F (174°C), take the smoked turkey out of the smoker.

7. Transfer the turkey to a flat surface then let it sit for about 15 minutes.

8. Cut into slices then arrange on a serving dish.

9. Serve and enjoy.

Chicken Breast with Wine

(total cook time 4 hours 10 minutes)

Ingredients for 10 servings

- Chicken (6-lbs., 2.7-kgs)

The Injection

- Butter – ½ cup

- Whine wine – 12 oz.

- Garlic powder – 1 teaspoon

The Fire

- Preheat the smoker an hour prior to smoking.

- Add charcoal and cherry wood chips during the smoking time.

- Soak the wood chips before using.

The Method

1. Preheat a smoker to 225°F (107°C).

2. Place the butter in a saucepan then melt over low heat.

3. Once the butter is melted, combine with garlic powder and white wine then mix until incorporated.

4. Fill the injector with the wine mixture then inject the chicken in several places—as many as possible.

5. Wrap the chicken with aluminum foil then prick in several places to let the smoke get into the chicken.

6. When the smoker is ready, place the wrapped chicken in the smoker.

7. Smoke the chicken for 4 hours. Check the internal temperature of the chicken. It should reach 165°F (174°C).

8. Once it is done, take the smoked chicken out of the smoker then let it sit.

9. Carefully unwrap the smoked chicken then transfer to a serving dish.

10. Cut into slices then serve.

11. Enjoy!

GOOSE BREAST

(TOTAL COOK TIME 9 HOURS 45 MINUTES)

INGREDIENTS FOR 10 SERVINGS

- Goose breast (5-lbs., 2.3-kgs)

THE RUB

- Low sodium soy sauce – 3 cups
- Molasses – ½ cup
- Brown sugar – ½ cup
- Red chili flakes – 1 ½ tablespoons

THE FIRE

- Preheat the smoker an hour prior to smoking.

- Add charcoal and nectarine wood chips during the smoking time.

- Soak the wood chips before using.

THE METHOD

1. Combine the soy sauce with molasses and brown sugar in a bowl.

2. Add red chili flakes then mix until incorporated.

3. Rub the goose breast with the mixture then place in a zipper-lock plastic bag. Marinate the goose breast overnight.

4. In the morning, remove the marinated goose breast from the refrigerator then thaw to room temperature.

5. Preheat a smoker to 225°F (107°C)—use indirect heat.

6. When the smoker is ready, place the marinated goose breast in the smoker.

7. Smoke the goose breast for 90 minutes or until the internal temperature has reached 140°F (60°C). Usually, the inside of the goose breast is still pink, but it is fine.

8. Take the smoked goose breast out of the smoker then let it rest for approximately 15 minutes.

9. Place the smoked goose breast on a flat surface then cut into slices.

10. Serve and enjoy.

Honey Duck with Black Tea

(TOTAL COOK TIME 5 HOURS 10 MINUTES)

INGREDIENTS FOR 10 SERVINGS

- Whole Duck (5-lbs., 2.3-kgs)

THE SPICE

- Black tea – 1 ½ cups

- Honey – ¾ cup

- Ginger – 1 tablespoon

- Chopped onion – 1 cup

- Cinnamon – 2 teaspoons

- Salt – ¼ cup

THE FIRE

- Preheat the smoker an hour prior to smoking.

- Add charcoal and nectarine wood chips during the smoking time.

- Soak the wood chips before using.

THE METHOD

1. Pour black tea into a bowl then stir in salt, cinnamon, and ginger. Mix until incorporated.

2. Add honey to the mixture then mix until the honey is completely dissolved.

3. Rub the duck with the mixture then place in a disposable aluminum pan.

4. Sprinkle chopped onion in the duck cavity then let it sit.

5. Place the charcoal and smoked nectarine wood chips in a smoker then preheat it to 225°F (107°C)—use indirect heat.

6. Once the smoker has reached the desired temperature, place the disposable aluminum pan with the duck on the smoker's rack.

7. Smoke the duck for 5 hours or until the internal temperature has reached 165°F (74°C).

8. Remove the smoked duck from the smoker then transfer to a serving dish.

9. Serve and enjoy the smoked duck with roasted vegetables.

CHICKEN WITH COFFEE AND BERRIES

(TOTAL COOK TIME 5 HOURS 10 MINUTES)

INGREDIENTS FOR 10 SERVINGS

- Whole Chicken (5-lbs., 2.3-kgs)

THE RUB

- Soy sauce – ¼ cup

THE SPICE

- Coffee beans – 1 ¼ cups
- Hot water – 1 cup
- Fresh strawberries – ½ cup

THE FIRE

- Preheat the smoker an hour prior to smoking.
- Add charcoal and maple wood chips during the smoking time.
- Soak the wood chips before using.

THE METHOD

1. Rub the chicken with soy sauce then let it sit for about an hour. Chill in the refrigerator to keep it fresh.

2. Meanwhile, grind the coffee beans until smooth.

3. Using a coffee maker or anything you have to combine the coffee with water then drain it.

4. Pour the coffee into a blender then add fresh strawberries to the blender. Blend until smooth and incorporated.

5. Preheat a smoker to 225°F (107°C)—use indirect heat. Don't forget to soak the wood chips before using.

6. When the smoker is ready, remove the chicken from the refrigerator then place in the smoker.

7. Smoke the chicken for an hour then take it out of the smoker.

8. Glaze the half-smoked chicken with the coffee and strawberry mixture then wrap with aluminum foil.

9. Prick the aluminum foil in several places—to make the smoke get into the chicken easier. Return the chicken back to the smoker.

10. Smoke the chicken for approximately 4 hours or until the internal temperature has reached 165°F (74°C).

11. Once it is done, remove the smoked chicken from the smoker then place on a flat surface.

12. Cut into slices then serve warm.

CHAPTER-6 GAME

PHEASANT WITH MAPLE SYRUP

(TOTAL COOK TIME 9 HOURS 10 MINUTES)

INGREDIENTS FOR 10 SERVINGS

- Whole Pheasant 4 (6-lbs., 2.7-kgs)

THE BRINE

- Brown sugar – 1 cup
- Salt – ½ cup
- Water

THE GLAZE

- Maple syrup – 4 cups

THE FIRE

- Preheat the smoker an hour prior to smoking.
- Add charcoal and maple wood chips during the smoking time.
- Soak the wood chips before using.

THE METHOD

1. Combine the brine ingredients in a container then stir until the brown sugar and the salt is completely dissolved.

2. Add the pheasants to the brine mixture then marinate for at least 4 hours. Store in the refrigerator to keep them fresh.

3. After 4 hours, remove the pheasants from the refrigerator then discard the brine. Set aside.

4. Place charcoal and maple wood chips in the smoker then preheat the smoker to 225 °F (107°C)—using indirect heat.

5. Once the smoker hits the desired temperature, arrange the pheasants on the smoker's rack then smoke for an hour.

6. Meanwhile, pour maple syrup into a saucepan then bring to a simmer. Remove from heat.

7. After an hour, take the pheasants out of the smoker then place each pheasant in a disposable aluminum pan.

8. Baste the pheasants with the maple syrup then return them back to the smoker.

9. Smoke the pheasants for another 4 hours and baste once every 30 minutes.

10. Continue to smoke the pheasants until the internal temperature has reached 165°F (74°C).

11. Remove the smoked pheasants from the smoker then transfer to a serving dish.

12. Serve and enjoy the smoked pheasants warm or cold.

Moist Elk Loin

(TOTAL COOK TIME 5 HOURS 30 MINUTES)

INGREDIENTS FOR 10 SERVINGS

- Elk loin (6-lbs., 2.7-kgs)

THE INJECTION

- Beer – 12 oz.

THE RUB

- Olive oil – ½ cup

- Black pepper – 2 tablespoons

- Salt – 1 tablespoon

- Minced garlic – 3 tablespoons

- Beef broth – 1 ¼ cups

THE FIRE

- Preheat the smoker an hour prior to smoking.

- Add charcoal and hickory wood chips during the smoking time.

- Soak the wood chips before using.

THE METHOD

1. Preheat a smoker to 225°F (107°C).

2. Inject the elk loin with the beer in numerous places then set aside.

3. Combine black pepper and salt in the bowl then pour beef broth into the bowl.

4. Stir in olive oil then add minced garlic. Mix well.

5. Rub the elk loin with the black pepper mixture then wrap with aluminum foil.

6. Place the wrapped elk loin in the smoker then smoke for approximately 5 hours. Check the smoke and add more charcoal and soaked wood chips if it is necessary.

7. Once the smoked elk loin is done and the internal temperature has reached 150°F and 66°C, remove it from the smoker.

8. Unwrap the smoked elk loin then transfer to a serving dish.

9. Serve and enjoy with roasted vegetables or other complements, as you desired.

Venison in Mushroom Sauce

(TOTAL COOK TIME **8** HOURS **30** MINUTES)

INGREDIENTS FOR **10** SERVINGS

- Venison steak (6-lbs., 2.7-kgs)

THE MARINATE

- Chopped mushroom – 2 cups

- Minced garlic – 2 tablespoons

- Diced onion – 1 cup

- Red wine – ¾ cup

- Low sodium beef broth – 3 cups

- Butter – ¼ cup

- Olive oil – 3 tablespoons

- Salt – 2 tablespoons

- Pepper – 2 teaspoons

THE FIRE

- Preheat the smoker an hour prior to smoking.

- Add charcoal and oak wood chips during the smoking time.

- Soak the wood chips before using.

THE METHOD

1. Melt butter in a saucepan then let it cool for a few minutes.

2. Pour red wine and low sodium beef broth into a container then stir in salt and pepper. Mix until the salt and pepper are completely dissolved.

3. Add melted butter and olive oil then stir well.

4. Stir in minced garlic, diced onion, and chopped mushroom then mix until combined.

5. Add the venison steak to the container then marinate for at least 6 hours.

6. After 6 hours, preheat the smoker to 225°F (107°C).

7. Then the venison steak out of the refrigerator. Leave the marinade in the refrigerator.

8. Once the smoker is ready, place the marinated venison steak on the smoker's rack.

9. Smoke the venison for 2 hours if you want a medium-rare doneness. At this doneness level, the internal temperature for your smoked venison steak is 140°F (60°C).

10. Once the smoked venison steak is ready, remove it from the smoker then quickly wrap it with aluminum foil. Let it sit for approximately 15 minutes.

11. Meanwhile, take the marinade from the refrigerator then pour into a saucepan. Bring to boil.

12. Once the marinade is boiled, reduce the heat then cook until thickened. Remove from heat.

13. Unwrap the smoked venison steak then transfer to a serving dish.

14. Drizzle the mushroom sauce over the smoked venison steak then sprinkle chopped celeries or parsley on top.

15. Serve and enjoy warm.

SPICED GROUSE

(TOTAL COOK TIME 4 HOURS 10 MINUTES)

INGREDIENTS FOR 10 SERVINGS

- Whole grouse 5 (6-lbs., 2.7-kgs)

THE RUB

- Salt - ¼ cup

- Black pepper – 3 tablespoons

- Sweet paprika – 3 tablespoons

- Brown sugar – ¼ cup

- Dried thyme – 2 ½ tablespoons

- Garlic powder – 3 tablespoons

- Onion powder – 1 ½ tablespoons

- Cayenne pepper – 2 teaspoons

THE FIRE

- Preheat the smoker an hour prior to smoking.

- Add charcoal and oak wood chips during the smoking time.

- Soak the wood chips before using.

THE METHOD

1. Combine salt with black pepper, sweet paprika, brown sugar, dried thyme, garlic powder, onion powder, and cayenne pepper in a bowl. Mix well.

2. Rub the grouses with the spice mixture then place in a disposable aluminum pan.

3. Preheat a smoker to 225°F (107°C)—use indirect heat.

4. Once the smoker is ready, arrange the rubbed grouses on the smoker's rack.

5. Smoke for approximately 4 hours. Regularly check the smoke and add more charcoal and wood chips if it is needed.

6. Once the internal temperature has reached 165°F (74°C), take the smoked grouses out of the smoker.

7. Place the smoked grouses on a serving dish then serve.

8. Enjoy!

CHAPTER-7
VEGETABLES

CARROTS

(TOTAL COOK TIME 25 MINUTES)

INGREDIENTS FOR 10 SERVINGS

- Medium carrots (2.5-lbs., 1.1-kgs)

THE SPICE

- Olive oil – 2 ½ tablespoons

- Smoked paprika – 2 teaspoons

- Salt – 1 teaspoon

- Black pepper – ¾ teaspoon

THE TOPPING

- Chopped fresh cilantro – 2 tablespoons

THE FIRE

- Preheat the smoker an hour prior to smoking.

- Add charcoal and apple wood chips during the smoking time.

- Soak the wood chips before using.

THE METHOD

1. Place charcoal and apple wood chips in the smoker then preheat the smoker to 225 °F (107°C)—using indirect heat.

2. Peel the carrots then place in a disposable aluminum pan.

3. Sprinkle salt, black pepper, and smoked paprika over the carrots.

4. Drizzle olive oil on top then toss to combine. Sprinkle chopped cilantro on top.

5. Wait until the smoker is ready then place the disposable aluminum pan in the smoker.

6. Smoke the carrots for 25 minutes or until the smoked carrots are tender.

7. Remove the smoked carrots from the smoker then transfer to a serving dish.

8. Serve and enjoy.

CAULIFLOWER

(TOTAL COOK TIME **2** HOURS)

INGREDIENTS FOR **10** SERVINGS

- Cauliflower (2.5-lbs., 1.1-kgs)

THE BRINE

- Salt – 2 tablespoons
- Water

The Spice

- Minced garlic – ¼ cup

- Olive oil – ¼ cup

- Smoked paprika – 2 tablespoons

- Lemon juice – 2 tablespoons

- Cumin – 1 teaspoon

- Cayenne pepper – 1 teaspoon

- Tomato puree – 2 tablespoons

The Fire

- Preheat the smoker an hour prior to smoking.

- Add charcoal and apple wood chips during the smoking time.

- Soak the wood chips before using.

The Method

1. Pour water and salt in a pot then stir until the salt is completely dissolved.

2. Add the cauliflower to the pot then soak for an hour--this will help to remove the insects from the cauliflower.

3. Preheat a smoker to 225 °F (107°C)—using indirect heat. Don't forget to soak the wood chips before using.

4. Meanwhile, combine minced garlic with olive oil, smoked paprika, lemon juice, cumin, cayenne pepper, and tomato puree in a bowl. Mix well.

5. After an hour, take the cauliflower from the brine then wash and rinse completely.

6. Rub the cauliflower with the spice mixture then place on the smoker's rack. The cauliflower should be smoked over a water tray.

7. Smoke the cauliflower for 20 minutes. Flip once every 5 minutes.

8. Once it is done, remove the smoked cauliflower from the smoker then let it sit for a few minutes.

9. Cut the smoked cauliflower according to the florets then place on a serving dish.

10. Serve and enjoy warm.

MIXED VEGETABLES

(TOTAL COOK TIME 3 HOURS 20 MINUTES)

INGREDIENTS FOR 10 SERVINGS

- Yellow squash – 3
- Medium zucchinis – 3
- Cherry tomatoes – 2 ½ cups
- Chopped onion – 2 cups

THE DRESSING

- Italian dressing – 1 ½ cups

THE FIRE

- Preheat the smoker an hour prior to smoking.

- Add charcoal and apple wood chips during the smoking time.

- Soak the wood chips before using.

THE METHOD

1. Cut the yellow squash into pieces then place in a zipper-lock plastic bag.

2. Cut the zucchinis into thick slices then also add to the same plastic bag with the squash.

3. Stir chopped cherry tomatoes and chopped onion into the zipper-lock plastic bag then drizzle Italian dressing over the vegetables.

4. Seal the plastic bag properly then shake until all of the vegetables are coated with the dressing.

5. Marinate the vegetables for 2 hours and store in the fridge to keep them fresh.

6. Preheat a smoker to 250°F (121°C).

7. Remove the vegetables from the fridge then transfer to a disposable aluminum pan. Drizzle the remaining liquid over the vegetables.

8. Once the smoker is ready, place the aluminum pan on the smoker's rack.

9. Smoke the vegetables for an hour or until tender.

10. Take the aluminum pan out of the smoker then transfer the smoked vegetables to a serving dish.

11. Serve and enjoy right away.

CONCLUSION

I can't express how honored I am to think that you found my book interesting and informative enough to read it all through to the end. I thank you again for purchasing this book and I hope that you had as much fun reading it as I had writing it. I bid you farewell and encourage you to move forward and find your true Smoked Meat spirit!

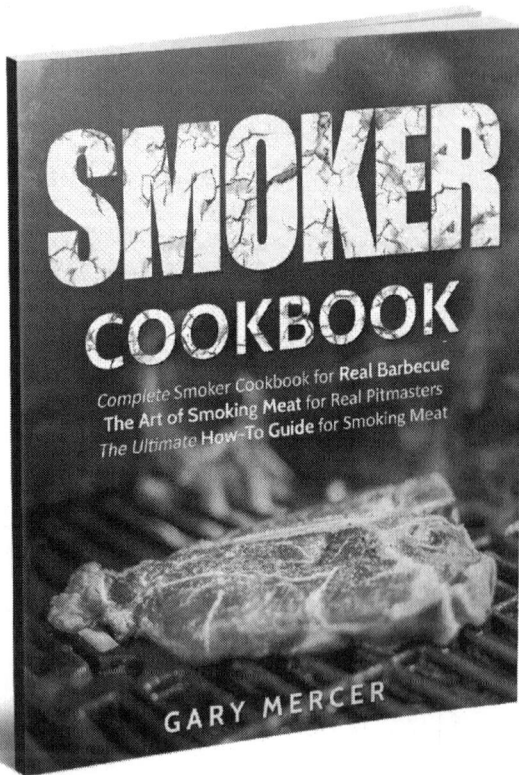

The ultimate how-to guide for smoking all types of meat, poultry, fish, and game. This book on smoking meats for beginners is the guide to mastering the low and slow art of smoking beef, fish, seafood, poultry, pork, vegetables, and game at your home. This guide is an essential book for beginners who want to smoke meat without needing expert help from others. This book offers detailed guidance obtained by years of smoking meat, includes clear instructions and step-by-step directions for every recipe. This is the only guide you will ever need to professionally smoke a variety of meat. From well-known beef brisket, the book includes delicate elk, turkey, venison, and pheasant smoked meat recipes.

OTHER BOOKS BY GARY MERCER

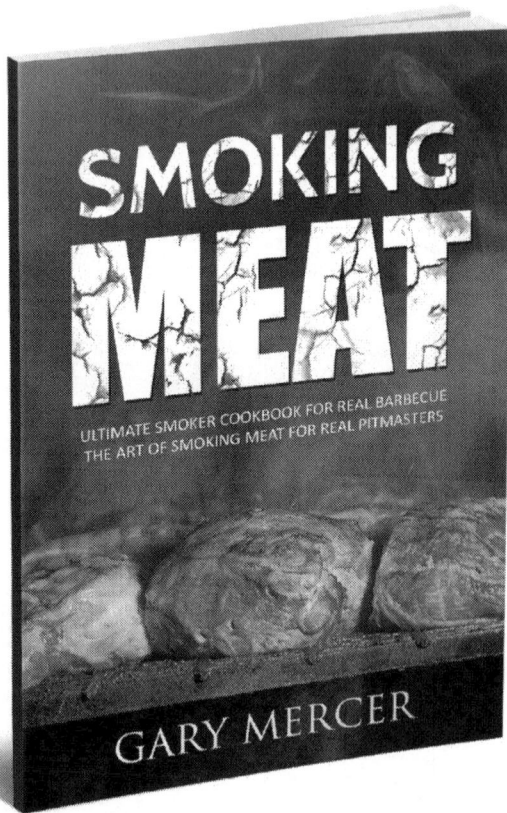

https://www.amazon.com/dp/1975935004

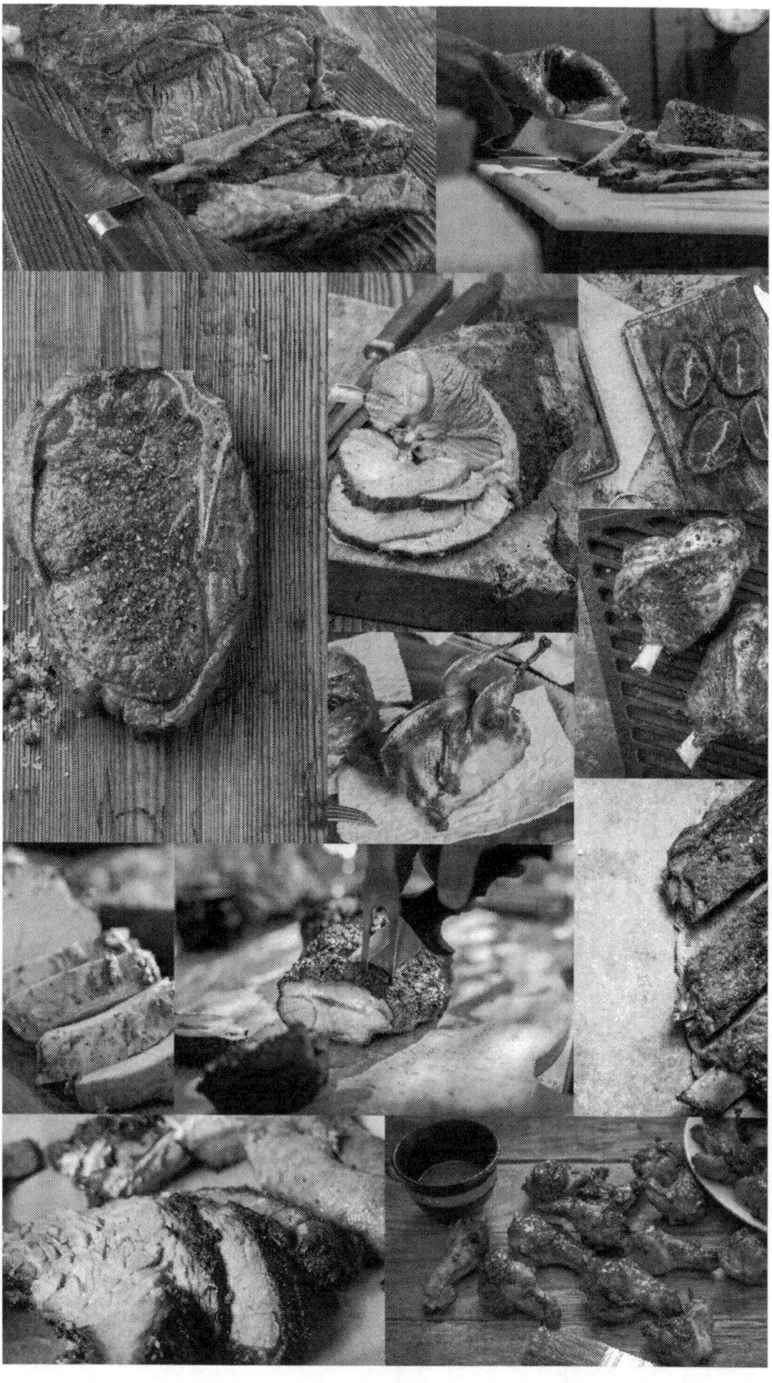

P.S. Thank you for reading this book. If you've enjoyed this book, please don't shy, drop me a line, leave a feedback or both on Amazon. I love reading feedbacks and your opinion is extremely important for me.

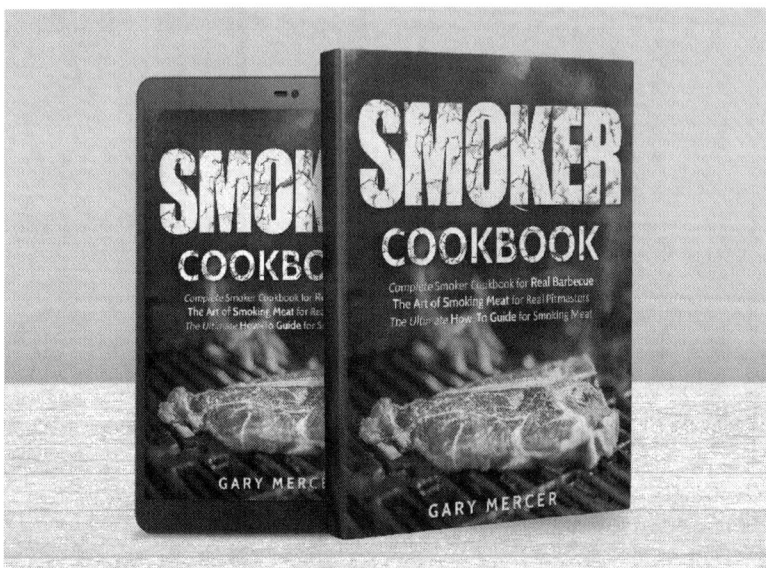

My Amazon page:

www.amazon.com/author/garymercer

Disclaimer and Terms of Use:*The effort has been made to ensure that the information in this book is accurate and complete, however, the author and the publisher do not warrant the accuracy of the information, text, and graphics contained within the book due to the rapidly changing nature of science, research, known and unknown facts and the internet. The Author and the publisher do not hold any responsibility for errors, omissions or contrary interpretation of the subject matter herein. This book is presented solely for motivational and informational purposes only.*

11987884R00057

Printed in Great Britain
by Amazon